HOW TO PASS
TECHNICAL
SELECTION
TESTS

MIKE BRYON · SANJAY MODHA

KOGAN
PAGE

Acknowledgements

We owe thanks to the many people who worked on the British Gas South Eastern project especially: Billy Seago, Derrin Schlesinger, Jon Stephenson and Gino Fox. Many thanks also to the employees of British Gas whose support made it possible.

First published in 1993, entitled *Technical Selection Tests and How to Pass Them* Reprinted and retitled 1994. Reprinted 1995, 1997 (twice), 1998, 2000

Kogan Page Limited
120 Pentonville Road
London N1 9JN

© Mike Bryon and Sanjay Modha 1993

419754
N15389

British Library Cataloguing in Publication Data

A CIP record for this book is available from the British Library.

ISBN 0–7494–0983–5

Typeset by DP Photosetting, Aylesbury, Bucks
Printed and bound in Great Britain by
Clays Ltd, St Ives plc

Contents

Introduction

Selection tests represent one of the greatest obstacles facing applicants for jobs, courses and apprenticeships in engineering.

Many applicants fail these tests or fail to show their true potential. They underperform because of, for example, nervousness or a lack of exam technique. Many candidates experience difficulty because they are unfamiliar with the way in which the questions are posed or simply because they are not practised in mental arithmetic. It is rare for use of a calculator to be allowed.

This book arose from a course developed for British Gas South Eastern. The course aimed to assist young people to demonstrate their true potential in the recruitment process for the Service Engineer apprenticeship. In particular, it aimed to assist students with the battery of selection tests used by British Gas.

It proved to be a considerable success with over 80 per cent of the students passing the tests. The contents of this book attempt to build on that success.

The course was awarded a regional commendation in the National Training Awards 1993.

The purpose of this book is to make available to a wider audience the techniques and strategies devised while preparing candidates for the selection tests of British Gas and other major employers.

Over half of the text comprises practice exercises which will make you feel more settled and confident. They may also improve your chances of passing and getting the job or career of your choice.

From our experience, doing well in a test is not only a matter of intelligence or aptitude but also requires confidence and determination. Many candidates fail to realise that you have to try hard to do well in a test.

If you are invited to undertake a selection test then you should set aside some time to go through the exercises in this book. You will find the answers to the practice questions at the end of each chapter.

Chapter 1
A Brief Guide to Tests

What are selection tests?

Tests have been used for many years now and are quite commonly referred to as selection tests. Selection tests, as the name suggests, are tests which are designed and used for the purpose of selecting and allocating people. The tests can be used in a number of situations; for example, in selecting for jobs, in promoting or transferring people to other departments or outplacement,* and in certain types of course and career counselling. These tests are known as psychometric tests, also sometimes called psychological tests.

Psychometric tests are one way of establishing or confirming an applicant's competence for the job. They can be useful provided they are *RELIABLE* and *VALID* for the job for which they are being used. Selection tests are standardised sets of questions or problems which allow an applicant's performance to be compared with that of other people of a similar background. For example, if you happen to be a graduate your score would be compared to those of other graduates, or if you have few or no qualifications your score would be compared to people who are similar to you, and so on. What this means is that the tests are *norm* referenced (the section dealing with Test scores (page 14) explains what is meant by norm referenced).

Do tests discriminate?

All good tests discriminate! That, after all, is the purpose of the test. However, this discrimination should be on the basis of

---

* Outplacement is a term used to describe a situation where a company wishing to make someone redundant provides help with finding another job.

ability. This is fair and legal discrimination. If the tests, or the way in which they are used, discriminate on the basis of sex or race then it would be unfair and possibly even illegal under the Sex Discrimination Act (1975) or the Race Relations Act (1976).

It does not matter whether the unfair discrimination is intentional or unintentional. However, the Acts do not explicitly refer to testing. The implication of the two Acts is that if the use of the tests (or other selection methods) results in proportionately more women or members of the ethnic minority communities 'failing' the test and as a result their application is rejected and the use of the test cannot be justified, then this may be unfair discrimination. The onus of proof is on the employer to justify the use of the test.

To put it another way, if an employer sets a condition (for example, a test score of X or above) and a larger proportion of women or members of ethnic minority groups fail to meet this condition, compared to men or the ethnic majority group, the employer may be required to show that this condition is an essential requirement. If the use of the test can be shown to be justified, the result would be fair discrimination.

When an employer uses tests to select future employees, it is on the understanding that the test will differentiate between those candidates with the appropriate skills, knowledge and potential and those without them or at a lower level. Since a test which does not differentiate levels of abilities between candidates is of no real value to the employer, it is important to the employer that the right person is chosen for the right job. It is equally important to the candidate that it is the right job for him or her. Otherwise the candidate may not be happy in the job; even worse, he or she may not be capable of doing the job, which can be very demoralising. In such a case they may have to look for another job and go through the whole selection process again.

So we can say that fair discrimination is about distinguishing between people based on their abilities and aptitudes, these must be shown to be related to the job for which the tests are being used. What this means in practice is that if an employer uses a particular test to identify a given set of abilities and aptitudes, these must be shown to be necessary to do the job. For example, it may need to be shown that high scorers do well in the job in question and that low scorers do not.

We mentioned the Sex Discrimination Act (1975) and the Race Relations Act (1976) earlier. These two Acts, which have a lot in common, have identified two types of discrimination: direct and indirect.

Direct discrimination is where an employer treats someone unfavourably because of his or her sex or colour or ethnic background. This type of discrimination is unlawful.

Indirect discrimination is where an employer sets a condition which a large proportion of a particular group fail to meet, eg women or people from ethnic minority groups. This type of discrimination could be held to be unlawful if the condition set by the employer is not necessary or justified.

Reliability and validity

We said that tests can be useful if they are reliable and valid. So what do these two words mean in this context?

Reliability

We can say that a test is reliable when consistent results are obtainable. For example, tests which contain ambiguous questions are likely to be unreliable because different people would interpret the questions differently or the same person may even interpret them differently on different occasions.

Validity

Tests are said to be valid when they measure what the employer/user wants them to measure. In personnel selection terms it means that a test must be related in some way to the known demands of the job if it is to be of any use. For example, it needs to be shown that a test score predicts success or failure in a given job.

Figure 1.1 illustrates the kind of relationship that ought to exist between test scores and job performance in which the higher the test score the better the performance in the job. In reality, however, it would be almost impossible to find such a

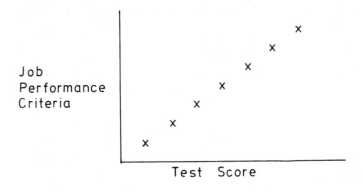

Figure 1.1 *A positive correlation between test scores and job performance*

high positive correlation. This is because of the difficulties in measuring job performance in many, if not most, types of job.

Why do companies use tests?

There are a number of advantages to companies and other organisations for using psychometric tests. These include:

1. Where an organisation receives a large number of applications, and because most selection tests are paper and pencil type, applicants can be tested in large groups. This is much more cost-effective than testing candidates individually.
2. The recruitment and selection process can be a very costly affair, particularly if there is a high turnover of staff because of bad selection decisions, not to mention any other disruptions that may be caused. Thus it is in the interest of the company to choose the right people for the job. The use of tests can help in this process, provided, of course, that the tests are both valid and reliable.
3. Tests can also lessen subjectiveness in assessing the applicant's potential to develop his or her aptitude for a particular job. The lessening of subjectiveness in the selection process is also an advantage for applicants.

Test administration

Most tests are conducted under strict 'examination' type conditions. The main reason for this is to ensure that all candidates, at all times, are tested in the same manner. This is done so that no group is either advantaged or disadvantaged in terms of receiving the test instructions or in the way in which the tests are conducted. For example, one group might be allowed extra time to complete a test and so have an unfair advantage. There is thus a high probability that this group's average scores will be higher compared to a similar group of people who did not have this unfair advantage.

The process that is followed will be laid down by the test publishers. However, the majority of tests are likely to be conducted in the following way:

1. All candidates will be sitting facing the test administrator.
2. Candidates will be provided with all the materials necessary, such as pencils, eraser, answer sheets.
3. The tester will explain the purpose of the test or tests and also inform candidates how the test will be conducted.
4. The tester will read the instructions that need to be followed for the test. These instructions may also be written on the test booklet, in which case you should read them at the same time. In some tests the candidates are left to read the instructions by themselves. The reading time may be included in the test time or extra time may be given.

   Whichever method is used, it is strongly advised that you read and understand the instructions. Our experience has shown that many candidates fail to understand the test instructions and therefore make many errors in completing the answer sheets. For example, some tests may require you to fill in *two* boxes on the answer sheet.
5. There will be a strict time limit. For the majority of tests, if not all, there is a time limit to which the tester will adhere. The tester may use a stop-watch; don't be put off by this. (Interest inventories and personality questionnaires do not usually have a strict time limit, though candidates are asked to complete them as quickly as possible.)

6. Many tests have example questions. In some tests the candidates are asked to attempt these, while others have them already completed. In any case, their purpose is to ensure that the candidates understand what is required of them. Once again, make sure that you understand what you have to do.

7. In most tests candidates will be given the opportunity to ask questions. If you do not understand what is required of you, you should seek clarification. You should not feel intimidated about asking questions, no matter how trivial the question may seem. The chances are there may be other people who have similar questions but who haven't plucked up enough courage to ask. So the motto is – ask; you have nothing to lose!

Test scores

So far we have discussed a number of issues concerning the background of tests. But now we need to address what happens once you have taken the test.

Naturally they are scored; that is, they are marked. Once scored, the correct answers are added together. The result is called a raw score. If there is more than one test then all the raw scores are noted. A set of tests is called a 'battery of tests'.

The raw score does not really mean anything on its own. This is because it does not tell us whether it is a good score or a bad score. For example, let us assume that candidate A gets 30 questions right out of a possible 50. So candidate A has a raw score of 30. If the test is easy and most people who are similar to him or her would have scored around 40, A's score is bad. On the other hand, if the test is a difficult one and most of the other people would only have scored around 20, candidate A's score is a good one.

Thus, for the scores to be meaningful we have to compare the individual's score with that of a similar group of people. We would then be able to say that, compared to those people, this individual is either average, above average or below average. We make this comparison by using what are called norm tables. Norm tables tell us how other people have scored on a test. The group with whom we would compare an individual's score is called a norm group and test norms are the norm group's scores. In a norm referenced test the raw scores are compared with a norm group.

Chapter 2

How to Prepare for Tests

Test publishers recognise that the candidate who has had lots of experience of selection tests has an advantage over a candidate who faces a test for the first time. The experienced or 'test wise' candidate is likely to: make fewer mistakes, better understand the test demands, be more confident, cope better with nerves, have developed a better test technique and be more likely to pass!

To counteract the advantage enjoyed by the test wise, test descriptions are provided and they usually include practice questions. The idea is that the motivated candidate can practise on these questions and, therefore, have the same advantage as someone who has taken the test or a similar test before. The problem is that there are nearly always too few practice questions for the candidate to prepare thoroughly.

This is the main reason why we have produced this book. We feel that test publishers provide insufficient practice material to allow candidates to brush up properly their skills and abilities and so demonstrate their true potential.

Practice makes perfect

You will find in this book many practice questions. They are designed to help you brush up the types of skill examined in selection tests. They will also help you to become familiar with the kind of question and the exam type conditions which apply in selection tests.

If you have to pass a sight test or if you need to pass a

medical examination or be a certain height to get a job then there is no way that practice can help you to achieve these requirements. It is clearly absurd to suggest, for example, that you can improve your height through practice.

However, if you have to pass a test of your command of maths, English or basic science then practice can make a difference. If you are new to tests or if you need to brush up your maths, English or basic science then you are most likely to see the biggest improvements in your score.

We cannot say for certain that if you practise you will pass a selection test. But why not look at it this way: If you have been asked to sit a test then you have nothing to lose and possibly everything to gain if you undertake some test practice. It will help you to feel more settled and confident. It might mean that you build up your speed and accuracy and help you to cope with any nerves. It will help you to demonstrate your true potential. It might mean you pass something you would otherwise have failed.

How best to practise

Education is the best sort of preparation for an employers' test. If you have just left full- or part-time study much of what you have done will have prepared you for these types of test.

Even if you have recently left education you can still benefit from practice. It will make you feel more settled about the test, and can also help you to brush up subjects which you may not have studied for some years. The most common of these is basic mental arithmetic. It is unusual for use of a calculator to be allowed in a selection test.

If it is some years since you undertook formal study or if you have done few or no employers' tests before then experience has shown us that up to 21 hours of practice can help.

The best type of practice is carried out on material which is very similar to the questions found in the real test. You should also try to get hold of material which allows you to practise on similar material under realistic test-type conditions.

If the test examines your command of basic science, the

vocabulary of science or maths, the material contained in this book will be of great benefit.

To be sure that you have the right kind of practice material you should read carefully the test description sent to you by the employer (if you have not received one then telephone and ask if they can provide you with details of the test).

Very often the test will be divided into sub-tests, each of which is separately timed and designed to measure a different ability. Make certain that you have practice material relevant to all the sub-tests.

If a selection of the test is not covered by the material in this book or if you want further material, you might obtain it from two other Kogan Page titles: *How to Master Selection Tests* and *Test Your Own Aptitude*. Other useful sources are books which purport to measure your IQ (intelligence quotient) and technical books with questions at the end of chapters. The careers service may also have suitable material.

Organise your study

The benefit of practice is short-lived so you need to start close to when you have the test and continue right up to the day before. Concentrate on the skills which you are least good at. Try to be honest with yourself. If, for example, maths is your weakness then spend most time practising to build up your speed and accuracy in calculations. If the test description includes an example of a type of calculation which you cannot do then make sure you are able to do them when the day of the test arrives. You should aim to do in total between 12 and 21 hours of practice.

Your programme of work should look something like this:

You are notified that you are going to have to sit the test.
You read the test description carefully.
You search for relevant test material.
You undertake a series of practice sessions.
You take the test.

Doing your best on the day

Go to bed early and try to get a good night's sleep. Do not drink alcohol. If you are unwell telephone the organisation and try to arrange to sit the test on another day. You will not need pens or paper as everything is supplied; however, it is important that you take with you your reading glasses or hearing aid if you wear them.

Leave home with plenty of time and go to the toilet before the test. Listen carefully to what the test administrator has to say. If you miss a point or do not understand something ask the administrator to repeat it.

It is highly likely that you will work through some practice questions before the real test starts. Don't worry if you get any of these examples wrong as they do not count towards your score. Make sure, however, that you realise what you did wrong. If there is anything you do not understand ask the administrator to explain it. Don't be shy as this is your last chance to have something explained to you. Once the test begins you will not be able to ask questions or get help.

Test strategies

During the real test it is very important that you do not waste time on questions to which you do not know the answer. If it is allowed, do all the easy questions first. Then, if you have time, go back to any questions you missed.

In multiple-choice papers,* if you are not sure which is the correct answer it may help if you can rule out some of the suggested answers as wrong and then make an educated guess.

Make sure you indicate the answer in the way requested. Do not, for example, tick or cross the correct answer if the instructions ask you to circle it.

If you are placing your answers on a separate sheet regularly

---

* Multiple-choice papers comprise questions which provide a number of suggested answers. Your task is to select the answer or answers which you believe to be correct.

check that you are placing your mark in the correct place. If, for example, you are doing question 9 make sure your answer is against the number 9 on the answer sheet.

Do not be surprised if you cannot answer all the questions in the given time. It is quite usual for there to be more questions than it is possible to answer.

Speed is of the essence so work as quickly as you can without rushing. This is where practice can really help.

In multiple-choice maths questions estimating sometimes helps. Instead of trying to work out the exact answer to sums you find difficult, round the amount up or down to the nearest whole number.

You have to try hard to do well in a test

We cannot stress this enough. It is not only a matter of intelligence or aptitude. Your frame of mind is just as important. Push yourself, keep going and concentrating until you hear the words 'Stop now, please'. You really have to go for it in a selection test. The person who will pass is likely to be the candidate who is sitting poised ready to start; you can almost see their determination as they turn the page and get down to the questions. At the end of the test if you do not feel drained by the exertion then you may not have done yourself justice.

What to do if you fail

Failing a test does not necessarily mean that you are incapable of doing the job or that you are not cut out for your chosen career. You may have failed by only one mark – that is how unfair these tests can seem. If you took the test again you might pass on your second attempt.

If you know what kind of career you want do not let a negative test result discourage you into giving up your dream. We know this is easy to say but we have seen so many people pass having previously failed and gone on to become perfectly good employees.

If you fail, get some advice. Go to your careers office or

adviser; they are happy to help people of all ages. And try to find out about qualifications or courses which will help you to acquire the skills you need.

The chances are that an employer will not be willing to discuss your score with you or let you retake the test straight away. Find out when you can next apply and in the mean time work on the parts of the test in which you felt you did least well.

Apply to other organisations who recruit for similar positions. It may be that they do not use a test in their recruitment process. Even if they do, you may well do better in their test as you will be becoming 'test wise'. Do lots of practice before you take another test.

Chapter 3

Some of the Most Common Types of Technical Tests

Categories of tests

Ability is the most common aspect of a candidate which is subject to testing, either in the form of paper and pencil tests or some practical exercise. These practical tests are sometimes referred to as performance tests or work sample tests. We talk about these on page 23.

Ability tests fall into two main categories: attainment tests and aptitude tests. Attainment is the candidate's current skills and knowledge. Aptitude is either having a talent for a particular skill or the potential to acquire it. It needs to be pointed out that the distinction between attainment tests and aptitude tests is not clear-cut. Therefore, a single test can be used to measure either attainment or aptitude.

Attainment tests

Attainment tests are those which seek to assess how much skill and knowledge an individual has. For example, an arithmetic test for cashiers measures attainment as long as it is used to measure arithmetic and not used to measure performance as a cashier.

From an employer's point of view an attainment test may provide a better assessment than simply looking at past records of achievements or non-achievements as the case may be. A standardised test of arithmetic or spelling may give a more reliable indication of relevant present ability than a comparison of school qualifications in maths or English.

From a candidate's point of view an attainment test score will say more to an employer than simply talking about their skills. This is particularly useful when the candidate does not possess many, or even any, qualifications.

Aptitude tests

Aptitude tests are used to predict the potential of an individual for a particular job or a course of study. However, as mentioned above, it is not easy to separate tests of potential from tests of attainment because all forms of test assess the person's current skills and knowledge. But the results of that assessment may then be used in a variety of ways. For example:

- to highlight the individual's strengths and weaknesses
- to provide career counselling
- to predict success in a job or course.

Work sample tests

Work sample tests can be described as a miniature version of the job in question. The tasks would encompass the main or major elements of a job. They are called work sample tests because that is the main purpose, and they are also practical. Hence they are sometimes referred to as performance tests.

Trainability tests

Another variation of the work sample test is the trainability test. Trainability testing is a method of assessing applicants' potential for learning new skills in a particular area.

Trainability testing is relatively common in technical positions which often require the use of a range of hand tools and techniques. It is important that you take notes when the task is either being demonstrated or instructions given.

The types of tests that you are most likely to encounter are:

Technical tests of verbal reasoning

These are about how well you understand ideas expressed in words and how you think and reason with words.

Examples of the types of question that may be asked

1. Fluid is to liquid as Vapour is to _____

   (a) solid (b) water (c) gas (d) dense (e) not given

In this question you have to find out the association between the two words underlined and then apply the same principle to find the answer for the third word. The answer in this case is (c) – gas – because fluid and liquid have similar meaning, just as vapour and gas do.

2. Fill in the missing word

   If you can see through something it means that it is _____.

   (a) opaque (b) transparent (c) vague (d) familiar
   (e) creative

3. Two magnets with the same poles facing each other will _____ each other.

   (a) repel (b) attract (c) expand (d) contract
   (e) not given

The answer to question 2 is (b) – transparent – and the answer to question 3 is (a) – repel.

Technical tests of numerical reasoning

Like the verbal reasoning tests, the numerical reasoning tests aim to identify strengths in understanding ideas expressed in numbers and how well you think and reason with numbers.

Examples of technical numerical questions

1. If five cathode ray tubes cost £400, how much does each one cost?

   (a) £100 (b) £90 (c) £80 (d) £70 (e) £60

2. If the sum of angles in a square is 360°, what is the size of each angle?

(a) 60° (b) 70° (c) 80° (d) 90°

3.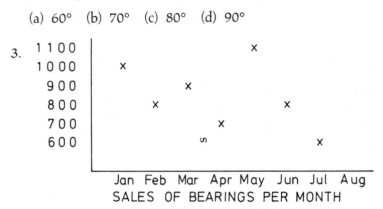

In which two months were the same number of bearings sold?

(a) Jan & Feb (b) Feb & Apr (c) June & Feb
(d) June & Apr (e) Apr & May

The answers to the above questions are:

1. (c) 2. (d) 3. (c)

Tests of diagram reasoning

In tests dealing with diagrams, you will be presented with shapes and patterns from which you have to work out some kind of logical sequence in order to answer the question. The format of the questions is likely to involve your being presented with five shapes or patterns with one of the figures missing. Underneath or beside these figures you will find a further five shapes or patterns from which you will have to select one as the missing answer. Look at the examples below.

Examples of diagram reasoning questions

1. OoOoO oOoOoO OoOoOoO oOoOoOoO ?

(a) oOoOoOoOo (b) OoOoOoOoO
(c) OoOOoOoOo (d) OoOoOoOo (e) OooOOooOO

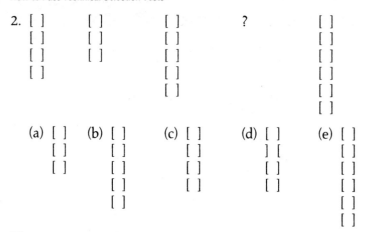

The answers are:

1. (b)   2. (c)

Tests of mechanical reasoning

Dealing with mechanical concepts (principles of transmitting movement).

Examples of mechanical reasoning questions

1. Which of the following will weigh the most: 1kg feathers, 1kg steel bar, 1kg stone?

   (a) the feathers   (b) the steel bar   (c) the stone
   (d) equal

2. In the diagram below, which switch(es) must be closed to light up the bulb?

   (a) 1   (b) 2   (c) 3   (d) all   (e) any one

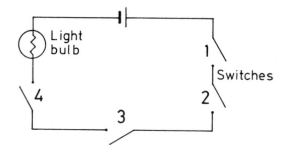

3. In which direction will B turn?

   (a) clockwise   (b) anti-clockwise   (c) will not turn

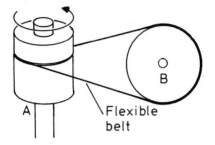

A   Flexible belt

The answers are: 1. (d)   2. (d)   3. (b)

The above list is not of course exhaustive. However, these are the main types of question that you are likely to come across under the heading of technical tests.

Chapter 4

Other Types of Test that You May Encounter

You will find that, regardless of the type of test you are taking, verbal and numerical tests will be part of the test battery. You will also find that the words and numbers used will relate to the type of job or course you are applying for. Thus for technical tests the majority of the words in the verbal section will be of a technical nature, whereas in a computer related test the words will be those used in computing, and so on.

Examples of other tests are:

Tests of clerical skills. These deal with checking and classifying data, speedily and accurately.

Tests of computer skills. These investigate the candidate's ability to follow set rules and instructions, sequence events into logical order and interpret flow charts.

Personality questionnaires. These aim to identify certain stable characteristics.

Interest inventories or interest blanks. These aim to identify an individual's interest in particular occupations.

Personality questionnaires (or tests)

Many people refer to personality inventories or questionnaires as tests. This, however, is misleading, since to talk about personality questionnaires as tests implies that there is a pass or fail score, which obviously is not the case.

It would appear that personality is something that everyone talks about. One often hears people talk about someone having a 'great personality', but what exactly is it?

There is no one theory or definition of personality with which all psychologists agree, but most personality questionnaires aim to identify certain stable characteristics. They are based on the assumption that the responses will be representative of how an individual will react in a given social situation, particularly the one in which the selector is interested, ie the organisation or department in which that individual may be working.

The main characteristics that personality questionnaires aim to identify in an individual are:

Extroversion	*Introversion*
Tough minded	Tender minded
Independent	Dependent
High self-confidence	Low self-confidence

Interest inventories (or tests)

Strictly speaking 'interest tests' like 'personality tests' are not tests at all, because they are not about obtaining a good or a bad score, nor about passing or failing. It is for this reason that they are usually referred to as interest inventories or interest questionnaires. The aim of these interest inventories is to find out an individual's interest in particular occupations.

Interest inventories would cover interests in activities such as:

- **Scientific/Technical** – how and why things work or happen.
    Types of job: different kinds of engineers and technicians.

- **Social/Welfare** – helping or caring for people.
    Types of job: youth/community worker, nursing,
        teacher/instructor, social worker.

- **Persuasion** – influencing people and/or ideas or selling
        goods and services.
    Types of job: salesperson, manager, advertising.

- **Arts** – designing or creating things or ideas.
  Types of job: writer, clothes designer, painter.

- **Clerical/Computing** – handling data, systems.
  Types of job: administrator, bookkeeper.

The use of interest inventories is limited compared to, say, aptitude tests in the selection of applicants. This is because the inventories appear, at least on the face of it, easy to fake. For example, if a person is applying for a position as a clerk, they may deliberately indicate a stronger interest in tasks related to the office environment.

The interest inventories are probably most useful in vocational guidance where, one assumes, that people are less likely, if at all, to fake them.

Chapter 5

The Technical Selection Tests Essential Dictionary

To do well in a technical test you must be familiar with the basic vocabulary of science and engineering. The best kind of practice comes from reading textbooks and discussing the subject in a classroom or at work. It will also help if you commit meanings to memory.

Below you will find approximately 100 words. It is essential that you know their meanings. All are taken from the basic vocabulary of technical subjects and often come up in tests.

The definitions offered are intended only as a reminder of the meaning. If you are new to any of them you may need to refer to specialist textbooks. Quick study guides and revision books for GCSE physics are especially useful.

Before you take a technical test make sure you know the meanings of the following words:

Abrasion   The effect on a surface of grinding by a hard or scraping substance.

Accelerator   The pedal or lever which increases the speed of a vehicle.

Adhesion   The sticking together of two or more surfaces.

Aerial   An object used for the transmission or receiving of radio waves.

Alloy   A mixture of two or more pure metals.

Alternating current   An electric current which flows alternately in one direction and then in the other.

Ammeter   The instrument used to measure electric current.

Anode   An electrode with a positive charge.

Arc   A curve, in particular, any part of the circumference of a circle.

Area   The space occupied by a surface.

Atmospheric pressure   The weight of all the air in the atmosphere. It changes according to how high you are and with the weather. Normally atmospheric pressure is taken to be the pressure of the air at sea level.

Axle   A spindle on which, or with which, a wheel or wheels revolve.

Balance   An instrument used to weigh objects.

Barometer   Instrument for measuring atmospheric pressure; used in the forecasting of weather and ascertaining height above sea level.

Battery   Electric cells connected together to provide current.

Beam   A horizontal strong point; for example, a joist used in the construction of floors and ceilings.

Bearing   A machine part used to reduce friction at the point where a rotating shaft and its support bear on each other. Types of bearing include, for example, plain, ball and roller.

Bimetallic   Two metals one on top of the other, bound together to form a strip.

Block and tackle   An arrangement of ropes or chains and pullies used to provide mechanical advantage in the lifting of heavy loads.

Brake   A device to slow down or stop a moving part or object.

Capacitor   A device used to accumulate electric charge.

Catalyst   A substance which aids a chemical change in other substances but does not undergo change itself.

Cathode   A negatively charged electrode.

Ceramic   An article of, for example, clay or porcelain

hardened by being baked; non-metallic materials which are hard, brittle and poor conductors.

Circle   A closed plane curve; a line which is always equidistant from a point; a round enclosure.

Circuit   An insulated path – often of copper – through which an electric current passes.

Circumference   The distance around the outside of a circle.

Cohesion   Sticking together, force with which molecules stick together; tendency to remain united.

Combustion   Destruction by fire; development of light and heat going with chemical oxidation of organic tissue.

Compound   Mixture of elements; substance consisting of two or more elements chemically united.

Concave   A term applied to lenses or mirrors which have a surface curved inwards.

Condensing   Reducing from gas or vapour to liquid.

Cone   A three-dimensional figure with a flat circular base tapering to a point.

Convex   A term applied to lenses or mirrors which have a surface curved outwards.

Coupling   A joint which allows objects to be linked together; a joint which ensures motion is transferred from one part to another.

Cross-section   The view of the surface formed when a three-dimensional object is cut across.

Cube   A three-dimensional square, a box, a solid contained by squares.

Cylinder   A three-dimensional shape with straight sides and a circular base, top and cross-section.

Density   Compactness of substance; how heavy it is; a measure by ratio between mass and volume.

Diameter   Measured by drawing a straight line from one side to the other of any body or geometric figure, for example a circle – the line must pass through its centre.

Direct current   Electric current flowing in one direction only.

Dissolve   Make or become liquid, especially by immersion in a liquid. Often this involves the dissolving of a solid into a liquid.

Dynamo   A machine which converts mechanical energy into electric energy by rotating coils of copper in a magnetic field.

Eccentric   Not precisely circular; for example, a cam deliberately off-centre used to push open valves is eccentrically mounted; idiosyncratic.

Efficiency   The amount of useful work performed, expressed in relation to the amount of energy expended.

Electrolysis   The process by which electric current passes through a liquid which conducts electricity.

Electron   One of the fundamental constituents of matter; a sub-atomic particle with a negative charge.

Element   A substance that cannot be divided into simpler substances by chemical means.

Energy   The capability of doing work.

Equilibrium   The state of balance – something which is balanced.

Expansion   Increase in volume caused by heat.

Friction   The resistance which a body meets when moved across another body or surface.

Fulcrum   Point on which a lever is placed to get purchase or on which it turns or is supported.

Fuse   In most cases a thin piece of metal with a low melting point which melts if subjected to an ampage above a known amount.

Gear   A toothed wheel used to transmit motion or change the direction or speed of motion.

Graph   A diagram illustrating two or more variables and the relation which exists between them.

Gravity   A force of attraction between items of separated matter; the falling of objects dropped; the property of having weight.

Gyrate   To move in a circular manner, to rotate.

Helix   A spiral curve; the thread of a screw is an example. A curve which winds around the outside of a cylinder.

Hexagon   A shape with six sides and six angles.

Horizontal   A line or object which is parallel to the horizon; level or flat.

Hydraulic   Liquids in motion; machinery operated by force transmitted through a liquid.

Insulate   Prevent or reduce the passage of electricity or heat.

Isometric projection   An engineer's drawing; a method for producing a three-dimensional representation of an object.

Latent   Hidden, concealed, existing but not manifest; for example, latent heat.

Lever   A bar or rod used to provide mechanical advantage. One point (the fulcrum) is fixed, another is connected to the force (weight) to be resisted or acted on and a third point is connected with the force (power) applied.

Lubricant   A fluid applied in order to reduce friction.

Machine   An apparatus for applying mechanical power; it will comprise several parts, each with a definite function.

Magnet   Iron or iron ore which attracts iron (iron-based materials) and points magnetic north and south when suspended.

Material Matter from which things are made, raw, unmanufactured.

Molecule The smallest portion to which a compound substance can be reduced without losing its chemical identity.

Obscure Indistinct, not clear, hidden, remote from observation.

Oscillate Move to and fro between two points.

Parallel Lines which are continuously the same distance apart, for example, railway lines.

Pendulum A weight mounted to swing freely under the influence of gravity.

Pentagon A five-sided figure with five angles.

Perpendicular Very steep, erect, upright.

Pivot Short shaft or pin on which something turns or oscillates.

Pulley A set of wheels set in a block used to change the direction of force or provide mechanical advantage.

Pyramid A three-dimensional figure with a square base and sloping sides which meet at a point or apex.

Radius Straight line from the centre to the circumference of a circle or sphere.

Reflect Throw back off the surface of a body, in particular heat, light and sound.

Shear A strain produced by pressure in a structure or substance.

Solid Of stable shape, of three dimensions, not a liquid or gas, not hollow.

Spindle Another word for axle and kingpin; a rod which rotates and is used to support, for example, wheels.

Spring A coil or hair usually metal which if compressed returns to its original shape.

Sprocket   A toothed wheel which is used to engage a chain on, for example, a bike.

Square   A four-sided figure with sides of equal length.

Switch   A device which opens or closes an electric circuit.

Synthetic   Man-made, made up of artificial compounds rather than those extracted from, for example, plants.

Tension   Stress caused by pulling on a bar or cord etc.

Thermometer   Instrument for measuring temperature.

Tolerance   An allowance for variation in the dimensions of a machine.

Torque   A turning force; any force which causes rotation.

Triangle   A three-sided figure with three angles.

Vacuum   Pressure below that of the atmosphere. In some cases the pressure within an enclosed space can be considerably below atmospheric pressure.

Vaporising   The changing of a liquid into a gas.

Velocity   Quickness, rate of motion, speed in a given direction.

Vibrate   Move to and fro, oscillate; move rapidly and unceasingly.

Volume   Solid content, bulk.

Wavelengths   A wavelength is the distance between the peaks or troughs of any two waves. Sound, light etc are transmitted in waves.

Work   A result of force moving an object in the same direction as the force. Machines do work.

X and Y-axes   The horizontal (X) and vertical (Y) axes on a two-dimensional graph.

Chapter 6

Technical Numerical Questions

Section one

Try the questions below under timed conditions. Allow yourself ten minutes and see how many questions you can do. It is likely that you will not be able to complete all the 30 questions in this time. Do not worry, as most tests are designed so that the majority of people do not complete all the questions in the time allowed.

You should not spend too long on any one question; instead move on and if there is time you can come back to any questions that you have not done. In this way you will avoid wasting time and therefore have a chance of attempting all the questions, some of which you will find easier than others; thus your score may be better than if you waste time on questions that are difficult for you.

Before you start make sure that you will not be disturbed and have a watch in front of you so that you can time yourself properly. Do not go over the ten-minute time limit.

Now turn over the page and begin the test.

1. If a set of five screwdrivers costs £4, how much does each one cost?

   (a) 50p (b) 60p (c) 70p (d) 80p (e) 90p

2. If 1 kilogram is equivalent to approximately 2.2 imperial pounds, how many pounds would there be in 5 kilograms?

   (a) 10 (b) 10.2 (c) 11.2 (d) 11 (e) 10.8

3. How many 100g steel bars would you have in 1kg?

   (a) 10 (b) 11 (c) 12 (d) 13 (e) 14

4. If 12 inches equals 1 foot, how many inches would there be in 5 feet?

   (a) 40 inches (b) 50 inches (c) 60 inches
   (d) 70 inches (e) 55 inches

5. If 10mm is equal to 1cm, how many millimetres are there in 50 centimetres?

   (a) 50mm (b) 500mm (c) 5000mm (d) 550mm
   (e) 50 000mm

6. If a train travels at 90 miles per hour, how many miles will it travel in 20 minutes?

   (a) 20 miles (b) 30 miles (c) 40 miles
   (d) 50 miles (e) 35 miles

7. If a manufacturing company employs 500 people of whom 20% are women, how many women work there?

   (a) 20 (b) 50 (c) 100 (d) 150 (e) 200

8. What is the ratio of women to men in the above company?

   (a) 1:2 (b) 1:3 (c) 1:4 (d) 1:5 (e) 1:6

9. Assuming that a printer can print 5 characters per second,

how many characters would it be able to print in 2 minutes?

(a) 300   (b) 500   (c) 600   (d) 700   (e) 900

10. Assume that you can print 400 words on a sheet of A4 size paper, how many A4 size sheets of paper would you need to print 6000 words?

(a) 10   (b) 13   (c) 15   (d) 18   (e) 20

11. If a 90 litre tank needs to be filled up using a hose pipe which allows water to flow at 2 litres per second, how many seconds would be needed to fill the tank?

(a) 180 seconds   (b) 90 seconds   (c) 45 seconds
(d) 22.5 seconds   (e) 11.25 seconds

12. If a lathe rotates at 600rpm, how many times does it rotate in 1 second?

(a) 60   (b) 40   (c) 20   (d) 10   (e) 5

13. If the above lathe is able to rotate at twice the speed, how many times would it be able to rotate in 1 second?

(a) 60   (b) 40   (c) 20   (d) 10   (e) 5

14. If a car tyre costs £19.95, how much would it cost for a set of four plus a spare tyre?

(a) £99.99   (b) £99.00   (c) £99.75   (d) £95.00
(e) £90.95

15. If a discount of 10% is given on the total cost on the above tyres, how much money will be saved?

(a) £9.99   (b) £9.90   (c) £9.97   (d) £9.50   (e) £9.09

16. Three computers need different circuit boards replaced on each one. The cost is £125, £150 and £175. What is the average cost per board?

(a) £450   (b) £250   (c) £150   (d) £125   (e) £175

17. A technical magazine subscription costs £36 per annum. What is the cost of a single magazine?

    (a) £5   (b) £4   (c) £3   (d) £2   (e) £1

18. What is the total area of the two rectangles?

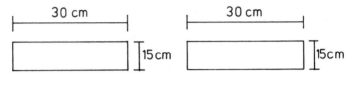

    (a) 450cm/sq   (b) 850cm/sq   (c) 950cm/sq
    (d) 900cm/sq   (e) 1800cm/sq

19. If a quarter of the box is shaded what percentage of the whole does that represent?

    (a) 20%   (b) 25%   (c) 30%   (d) 35%   (e) 40%

20. An electric saw turns at a speed of 120 revolutions per minute. How many revolutions will it have made at the end of 15 minutes?

    (a) 1200   (b) 1400   (c) 1600
    (d) 1800   (e) 2000

21. A train covers 380 miles in 4 hours, what would its average speed have been?

    (a) 80mph   (b) 85mph   (c) 90mph   (d) 95mph
    (e) 75mph

22. An electric water pump is able to pump water at a rate of

12 gallons per minute. How long would it take to fill a 900 gallon tank?

(a) 1hr (b) 1hr 30mins (c) 1hr 15mins (d) 2hrs (e) 45mins

23. What is the combined area of the rectangles below?

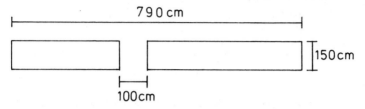

(a) 1.50m/sq (b) 13.35m/sq (c) 7.90m/sq
(d) 11.85m/sq (e) 10.35m/sq

24. See graph below. If the income from the sale of cars was £28 000, how many cars must have been sold?

(a) 25 (b) 30 (c) 35 (d) 40 (e) 45

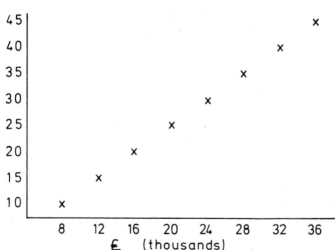

25. See graph above. If a salesperson gets 10% commission on all their sales, how much commission can be earned if 20 cars are sold?

(a) £120 (b) £160 (c) £1200 (d) £1600 (e) £16 000

26. Assume a lorry is able to hold a load of 350kg. If a load of only 175kg is put on the lorry, what percentage of its total capacity is being wasted?

    (a) 35%   (b) 40%   (c) 45%   (d) 50%   (e) 55%

27. An electric fan rotates at 70rpm at speed setting 1 and rotates at 120rpm at speed setting 2. What is the difference in speed in rpm between the two?

    (a) 70rpm   (b) 65rpm   (c) 60rpm   (d) 55rpm
    (e) 50rpm

28. At speed setting 3 the above fan rotates at 180rpm. How much faster is speed setting 3 in relation to speed setting 2, expressed as a percentage?

    (a) 50%   (b) 33%   (c) 60%   (d) 40%   (e) 66%

29. A computer operator is able to input 120 characters per minute using a standard keyboard. How many characters can be typed in half an hour?

    (a) 360   (b) 3600   (c) 36 000   (d) 1200   (e) 12 000

30. If a computer floppy disk is able to hold 720 000 characters, how many characters would 10 disks hold?

    (a) 720 000   (b) 72 000   (c) 7 200 000   (d) 14 000 000
    (e) 14 200 000

Section two

It is unlikely that you will be allowed to use a calculator in a test so if you rely on one undertake lots of practice to build up your speed and accuracy in mental arithmetic. Only use a calculator to check your answers.

So many people fail maths tests not because they are unable to do the questions but because they cannot do them quickly enough or because they make too many avoidable mistakes.

Practice will make the difference between pass and fail for these candidates.

You may need to learn or re-learn your multiplication tables.

Practice maths

Work out the number or symbols which complete each sum and write your answer in the box.

1. $9 - 3.6 + 4 = ?$

Answer

2. $? = 7 \times 38$

Answer

3. $? \times 6 = 20 + 16$

Answer

4. $158 - 6 = 129 + ?$

Answer

5. 102 – 96 = 18 ÷ ?

Answer

Fact: To convert inches to centimetres you multiply by 2.54.

6. How many centimetres are there in 50 inches?

Answer

7. 2.4 × 6.6 = ?

Answer

8. 3 ? 2.1 = 9.3 – 3
(Clue: Your answer should be either: plus, minus, divide or multiply)

Answer

9. 30% of 70 = ?

Answer

10. ? = 27 × 36

Answer

11. 7 + 2 = 17 ? 8

Answer

Fact: To convert grams to pounds you multiply by 0.0022.

12. How many pounds are equivalent to 5000 grams?

Answer

13. How many grams are there in 2.2 pounds?
(Clue: in this case you divide by 0.0022)

Answer

Work out the following and place your answer in the box.

14. 68 × 0.7 = ?

Answer

15. $7 \times 16 = 28 \times ?$

Answer

16. 40% of $30 = ?$

Answer

17. $5.5 \times 6 = 330 \div ?$

Answer

18. $300 - ? = 7 \times 16$

Answer

19. $26 - ? = 9.3$

Answer

20. 35 ? 17 = 95 + 500

Answer

Fact: To convert imperial tons to kilograms you multiply by 1016.

21. How many kilograms are there in an imperial ton?

Answer

22. How many kilograms are there in 7 imperial tons?

Answer

Fact: To convert gallons to litres you multiply by approximately 4.5.

23. Approximately how many litres of water are required to fill a 5 gallon bucket?

Answer

24. Approximately how many gallons are equivalent to 18 litres?

Answer

Some tests require you to demonstrate that you can deal with metric measurements. Try the following examples (express all answers in centimetres).

Fact: 10 millimetres (mm) = 1 centimetre (cm); 100 cm = 1 metre (m).

25. 10cm + 3m + 16mm = ?

Answer

26. 5cm – 7mm + 1m = ?

Answer

27. 22mm + 6cm + ? = 2m

Answer

28. 215mm – 5cm + 1.5m = ?

Answer

29. ? + 100cm + 16mm = 2.5m

Answer

30. 5 × 3m lengths of wood – ? = 2400mm

Answer

Practice test

Over the page you will find a mock test comprising 10 questions. Check your watch and give yourself three minutes.
   Do not turn the page until you are ready.

1. $86 - 14 = 9 + ?$

Answer

2. $23 + 18 = ? + 6$

Answer

3. $5 ? 1 = 20 \div 5$

Answer

4. $16 + 75 \div 7 = ?$

Answer

5. $? + 68 = 16 \times 9$

Answer

6. 9 × ? = 63

Answer

7. ? × 12 = 48

Answer

8. 45% of 70 = ?

Answer

9. 47 × 19 = ?

Answer

10. 9 × 6 + 33 = 3 ? 8 + 76

Answer

Answers

Chapter 6: Technical numerical questions

Section one (page 39)

1. (d)	2. (d)	3. (a)	4. (c)	5. (b)	6. (b)
7. (c)	8. (c)	9. (c)	10. (c)	11. (c)	12. (d)
13. (c)	14. (c)	15. (c)	16. (c)	17. (c)	18. (d)
19. (b)	20. (d)	21. (d)	22. (c)	23. (e)	24. (c)
25. (d)	26. (d)	27. (e)	28. (a)	29. (b)	30. (c)

Section two (page 44)

1. 9.4	11. – (Minus)	21. 1016
2. 266	12. 11	22. 7112
3. 6	13. 1000g	23. 22.5 (Approx)
4. 23	14. 47.6	24. 4 (Approx)
5. 3	15. 4	25. 311.6cm
6. 127	16. 12	26. 104.3cm
7. 15.84	17. 10	27. 191.8cm
8. × (Multiply)	18. 188	28. 166.5cm
9. 21	19. 16.7	29. 148.4cm
10. 972	20. × (Multiply)	30. 1260cm

Practice test (page 51)

1. 63	5. 76	9. 893
2. 35	6. 7	10. + (Plus)
3. – (Minus)	7. 4	
4. 13	8. 31.5	

Chapter 7
Technical Verbal Questions

This chapter comprises practice examples of the types of question which test your command of the basic vocabulary of science and engineering.

For some of the questions we have suggested time limits so that you can practise against the clock.

If you have learnt the essential dictionary (Chapter 5) you should be able to answer many of these questions.

The first eight questions test your knowledge of synonyms (words that mean the same).

1. Which of the following words means the same as eccentric?

   A normal   Answer
   B dull
   C idiosyncratic
   D energetic
   E none of these

2. Which of the following words means the same as corrode?

   A correspond   Answer
   B protect
   C rust
   D insulate
   E corrupt

3. Which of the following words means the same as sequence?

A series   Answer
B sequel
C random
D secretive
E disorder

4. Which of the following words means the same as variable?

A striped   Answer
B constant
C stable
D changeable
E steady

5. Which of the following words means the same as flexible?

A stiff   Answer
B pliable
C current
D immovable
E hollow

6. Which of the following words means the same as compress?

A condense   Answer
B spread
C impress
D expand
E pressure

7. Which of the following words means the same as saturate?

A dry   Answer
B gratify
C soak
D rainfall
E heat

8. Which of the following words means the same as invert?

A shy   Answer
B transpose
C equilibrium
D straighten
E transport

Over the page you will find two more of these types of question. Check your watch and allow one minute to complete them.

Do not turn the page until you are ready.

9. Which of the following words means the same as fluctuate?

A smooth   Answer
B vary
C liquid
D immobile
E level

10. Which of the following words means the same as precise?

A unclear   Answer
B guess
C accurate
D wrong
E none of these

The following types of question test your knowledge of the vocabulary of science by posing straightforward multiple-choice questions.

11. When light enters glass and changes direction this bending of light rays is called?

A reflection   Answer
B absorption
C transmission
D refraction
E deviation

12. Stored energy waiting to do work is called?

A potential energy   Answer
B inert energy
C kinetic energy
D nuclear energy

13. Speed in a stated direction is called?

A distance
B vectors
C newtons
D gradient
E acceleration

Answer

14. The flow of heat through a material without the material itself moving is called?

A insulation
B refraction
C reflection
D bimetallic
E conduction

Answer

15. When atoms of different elements link they form?

A neutrons
B protons
C molecules
D magnets
E solids

Answer

Over the page you will find two more of these types of question. Check your watch and allow one minute to complete them.

Do not turn the page until you are ready.

16. The measure of the amount of matter in an object is called the:

    A kilogram   Answer
    B atoms
    C volume
    D mass
    E area

17. A push or pull which one object applies to another is called a:

    A force   Answer
    B mass
    C velocity
    D physics
    E density

With the next type of question you have to choose a word from the suggested answers which best completes the sentence.

You are sometimes offered the answer 'None of these'; you select this if you believe none of the other answers is correct.

Choose the word which best completes the following sentences:

18. Electrons have a _____ charge.

    A positive   Answer
    B magnet
    C negative
    D neutron
    E massive

19. An electrical fuse is a short thin piece of _____.

    A current   Answer
    B wire
    C pipe
    D power
    E liquid
    F none of these

20. A _____ object is said to be in equilibrium.

    A heavy   Answer
    B clockwise
    C balanced
    D gravity
    E pivot

21. _____ is needed to change liquid into vapour.

    A insulation   Answer
    B velocity
    C cold
    D heat
    E gas

22. Steam _____ to form water.

    A evaporates   Answer
    B melts
    C condenses
    D boils
    E fuses

23. Each moving or vibrating molecule has _____ energy.

    A kinetic   Answer
    B random
    C molecular
    D microscopic

24. Friction is the _____ a body meets when moving across another body or surface.

    A energy   Answer
    B efficiency
    C resistance
    D mass
    E law

25. A body gyrates when it moves in a _____ manner.

    A constant   Answer
    B circular
    C straight
    D vertical
    E lively

26. _____ prevents or reduces the passage of electricity or heat.

    A insulation   Answer
    B a pivot
    C hydraulics
    D a magnet
    E a dynamo

27. The rate of _____ of a body is called its velocity.

    A vibration   Answer
    B reflection
    C work
    D resistance
    E motion

28. A substance which aids a chemical change in other bodies but does not undergo change itself is called a _____.

    A gas   Answer
    B bimetallic
    C catalyst
    D synthetic
    E category

29. An alloy is a mixture of two or more pure _____.

    A metals   Answer
    B liquids
    C substances
    D solids
    E gases

Over the page you will find five more of these types of question. Check your watch and allow two minutes to complete them.

Do not turn the page until you are ready.

30. _____ pressure changes depending on how high you are and with the weather.

    A barometer   Answer
    B electrical
    C work
    D gravitational
    E atmospheric

31. When an object is _____ its molecules vibrate violently.

    A frozen   Answer
    B obscure
    C heated
    D circular
    E stretched

32. _____ zero is the lowest possible temperature which can be reached.

    A Kelvin   Answer
    B centigrade
    C absolute
    D freezing
    E cold

33. _____ is a body's power of doing work by virtue of its motion.

    A safety   Answer
    B vitality
    C friction
    D density
    E energy

34. In an element all atoms are _____.

    A identical   Answer
    B molecules
    C stretched
    D gases
    E idiosyncratic

35. Evaporation occurs at the _____ of a liquid.

    A surface   Answer
    B throughout
    C molecules
    D boiling-point
    E none of these

Until they get used to them, most people have difficulty with the next type of question.

You have to work out the relationship which exists between the first pair of words and then apply that relationship to the third word and the suggested answers.

We have provided you with an example below. In this instance the relationship between change and stability is that they are opposites so you have to look for the opposite of 'special' which is 'mundane'.

The relationship is not always one of opposites; it could be, for example, that they mean the same or one is a quality of the other.

We have given you over 30 practice questions so that you can undertake lots of practice.

Example:

36. Change is to stability as special is to:

    A multiple   Answer
    B particular
    C mundane   C
    D progress
    E peculiar

37. Car is to petrol as cooker is to:

    A battery   Answer
    B heat
    C food
    D gas
    E kitchen

38. Square metres are to area as cubic metres are to:

    A velocity   Answer
    B length
    C distance
    D height
    E volume

39. Clockwise is to anti-clockwise as forward is to:

    A vector   Answer
    B opposite
    C reverse
    D upwards
    E equilibrium

40. North Pole is to South Pole as anode is to:

    A cathode   Answer
    B positive
    C diode
    D negative
    E magnet

41. Frequency is to hertz as energy is to:

    A metre   Answer
    B work
    C joule
    D degree
    E watt

42. Screwdriver is to screw as hammer is to:

    A spanner   Answer
    B nail
    C cog
    D plug
    E mallet

43. Ohm is to resistance as watt is to:

    A volt
    B pressure
    C force
    D amplification
    E power

Answer

44. Ball is to sphere as box is to:

    A triangle
    B square
    C circle
    D cube
    E solid

Answer

45. Sphere is to circle as cube is to:

    A box
    B rectangle
    C square
    D house
    E none of these

Answer

46. Hurricane is to wind as monsoon is to:

    A tropics
    B storm
    C rain
    D sunshine
    E none of these

Answer

47. Wallet is to bank as shopping bag is to:

    A supermarket
    B cashpoint
    C vegetables
    D building society
    E none of these

Answer

48. Body is to blood as engine is to:

    A car   Answer
    B muscles
    C combustion
    D oil
    E none of these

49. Straight is to crooked as intact is to:

    A symmetrical   Answer
    B broken
    C horizontal
    D complete
    E none of these

50. See-through is to transparent as intact is to:

    A glass   Answer
    B opaque
    C drink
    D complete
    E none of these

51. Water is to irrigate as light is to:

    A illuminate   Answer
    B electricity
    C bulb
    D river
    E none of these

52. Centimetre is to ruler as ounce is to:

    A inch   Answer
    B scales
    C pound
    D rubber
    E none of these

53. Fat means the opposite of:

    A wide
    B thin
    C big
    D short
    E none of these

Answer

54. Straight means the opposite of:

    A long
    B flat
    C horizontal
    D bent
    E none of these

Answer

55. Frozen means the opposite of:

    A solid
    B melted
    C water
    D ice
    E none of these

Answer

56. Constant means the opposite of:

    A intermittent
    B continuous
    C often
    D always
    E none of these

Answer

57. Nervous means the opposite of:

    A confident
    B scared
    C cautious
    D silent
    E none of these

Answer

58. Effervescent means the opposite of:

    A bubbly
    B turbulent
    C pocket
    D tasty
    E still

Answer

59. Gram is to kilogram as metre is to:

    A length
    B kilometre
    C mile
    D ruler
    E speed

Answer

60. Kilometres per hour are to speedometer as degrees centigrade are to:

    A weather
    B heat
    C thermometer
    D Fahrenheit
    E miles

Answer

61. Second is to minute as day is to:

    A hour
    B week
    C night
    D clock
    E millisecond

Answer

62. Circle is to sphere as square is to:

    A pyramid
    B plane
    C triangle
    D rectangle
    E cube

Answer

Over the page you will find six more examples of this type of question. Check your watch and allow yourself three minutes to complete them.

Do not turn the page until you are ready.

63. Kilojoules are to energy as hectares are to:

    A area

    B electricity

    C agriculture

    D volume

    E current

Answer

64. Second is to time as litres are to:

    A space

    B solids

    C volume

    D fluid ounces

    E atoms

Answer

65. Millibars are to pressure as degrees centigrade are to:

    A temperature

    B weather

    C barometer

    D velocity

    E wind

Answer

66. Metre is to distance as watt is to:

    A volt

    B power

    C second

    D time

    E momentum

Answer

67. Condense is to cool as evaporate is to:

    A heat

    B liquid

    C freeze

    D solid

    E cool

Answer

68. One is to two as radius is to:

A diameter
B circumference
C three
D angle
E circle

Answer

Answers are on page 96.

Chapter 8

Tests of Diagram Reasoning

Diagram reasoning tests require you to find a missing shape or pattern from a set of figures that form a logical sequence. Diagram tests are also referred to as abstract reasoning tests because they do not have any verbal or numerical content, apart from the instructions. In other words, all the questions are picture (shapes and patterns) based, with no words or numbers.

Here you will find diagram reasoning example questions followed by a timed exercise.

Tests of diagram reasoning

You will be presented with shapes and patterns from which you have to work out a logical sequence of events in order to answer the question. The format of the question is likely to be that you are presented with five shapes or patterns with one of these figures missing. Underneath or beside these figures you will find a further five shapes or patterns from which you will have to select one as the missing answer. Here are two examples for you to consider:

Example questions

1. [ ]   [ ]   [ ]   ?   [ ]
   [ ]   [ ]   [ ]   [ ]
              [ ]   [ ]   [ ]
                         [ ]   [ ]
                                             [ ]
                                             [ ]

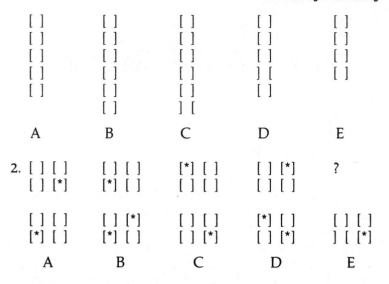

2.

Answers to the example questions are:

1. A   2. C.

On the next page you will find 19 diagram reasoning questions. You should attempt to do these in five minutes, so before you start make sure that you will not be disturbed and also make sure that you have a clock or a watch so that you can time yourself.

Also, ensure that you understand what is required of you; if not look at the above examples again. Once you have started, work as fast as you can and don't spend too long on any one question.

When you are ready start the test.

1.

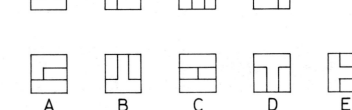

2.

3.

4.

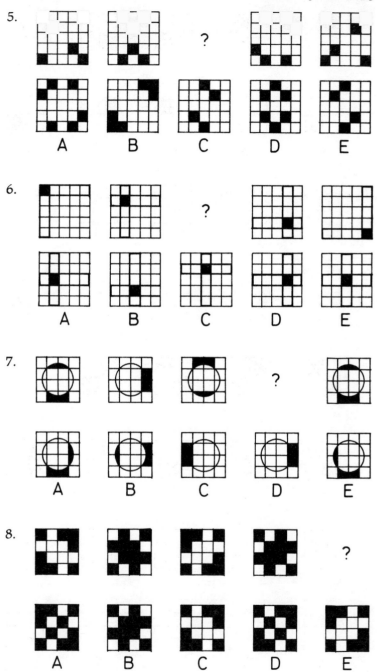

5.

6.

7.

8.

A   B   C   D   E

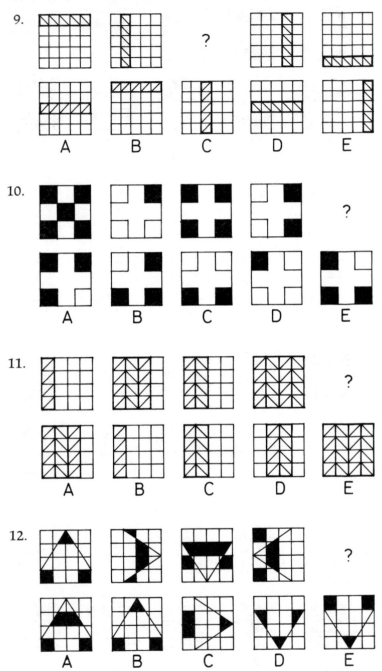

9.

10.

11.

12.

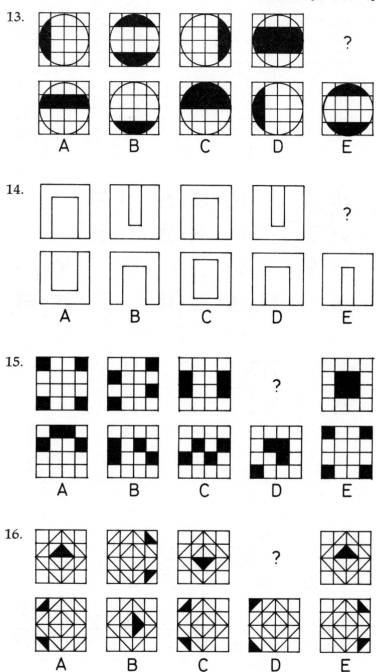

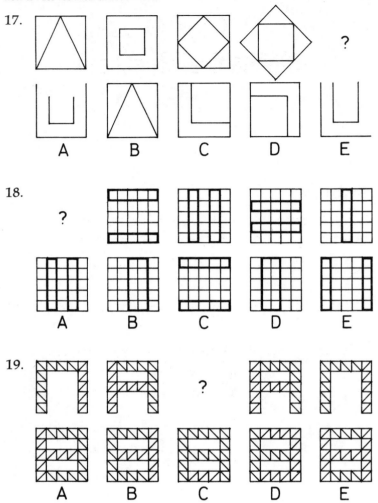

Answers are on page 96.

Chapter 9
Mechanical Questions

Section one

The questions in this section are based on the principles of mechanics, that is how things work and function.

Example questions

1. If B turns in an anti-clockwise direction which way will A turn?

   (a) Clockwise   (b) Anti-clockwise   (c) Not given

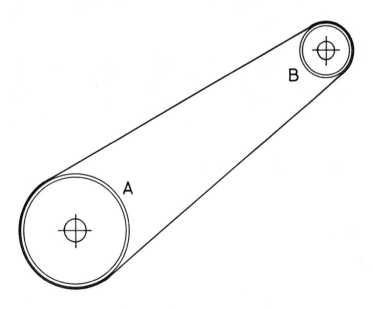

2. If a person facing North turns 90 degrees clockwise, what direction will that person be facing?

   (a) North   (b) East   (c) West   (d) South

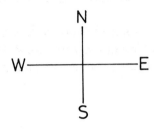

Answers to the example questions are:

1. (b)   2. (b).

Over the page you will find 15 mechanical reasoning test questions. These should be done to a strict time limit. You should try and do as many as you can in five minutes.

Remember to make sure that you won't be disturbed in the middle of the test and also be certain to time yourself accurately.

You should work as quickly and as thoroughly as you can, but don't spend too long on any one question.

When you are ready, turn over the page and begin.

1. Which switch(es) would you need to close to light up the bulb?

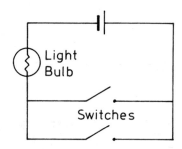

(a) C   (b) D   (c)   Either

2. If the left-hand side wheel rotates in the direction shown, which way will the other wheel turn?

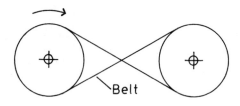

(a) Same direction   (b) Opposite direction
(c) Won't turn

3. Which point will balance the plank?

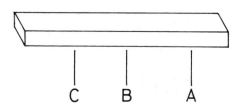

(a) C   (b) B   (c) A

4. If a person facing South turns 180 degrees in a clockwise direction, which way will that person be facing?

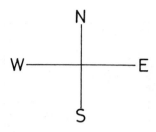

(a) North (b) East (c) West (d) South

5. If you were facing South and turned 360 degrees, what direction would you be facing?

(a) North (b) East (c) West (d) South

6. Which circuit has a serial connection?

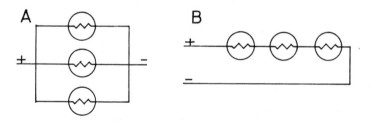

(a) A (b) B (c) Neither

7. What will happen to the two horse-shoe magnets? Will they _____

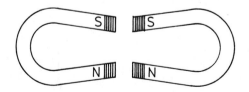

(a) Attract each other   (b) Repel each other
(c) Not given

8. If you wanted A to turn in a clockwise direction, which way would B have to rotate?

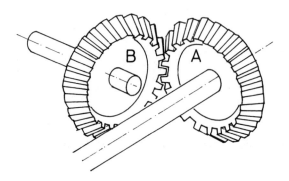

(a) Anti-clockwise   (b) Clockwise
(c) Same direction as gear A

9. Which chain is bearing the most stress of the weight?

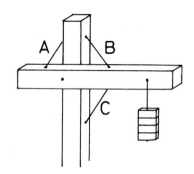

(a) A   (b) B   (c) C   (d) All equally

10. Which of the following statements is true?

(a) Smaller crank
Smaller movement
Easy to turn
(b) Bigger crank
Bigger movement
Easy to turn
(c) Size is not important

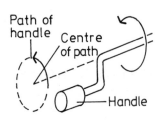

11. If a magnet is placed as shown, in which direction will the compass needle point?

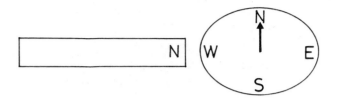

(a) East (b) West (c) North (d) South

12. Which pair of magnets will attract one another?

(a) A
(b) B
(c) C

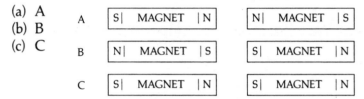

13. If gear B rotates in a particular direction, which direction, in relation to each other, will A and D rotate?

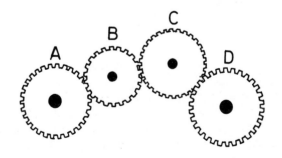

(a) In same direction as each other
(b) In opposite direction to each other
(c) Always clockwise
(d) Always anti-clockwise

14. By looking through this, objects will appear _____

Magnifying glass

(a) Smaller   (b) Bigger   (c) Same size

15. A rotates in the opposite direction to C; B rotates anti-clockwise. In which way will D turn?

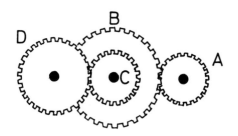

(a) Clockwise   (b) Anti-clockwise   (c) Same as C

Section two

Below are some more practice mechanical questions for which we have not suggested any time limits. Go over carefully any you get wrong. If there are some you do not understand it often helps to discuss them.

Try to make sure you understand the principle on which the question is based. You may need to undertake further reading. We would recommend any of the quick study or teach yourself physics books. For details ask at your local bookshop or library.

A

 B

Star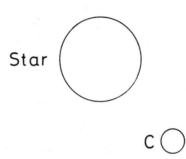

C ◯

16. Which planet will have the longest orbit of the star?

1.	2.	3.	4.
Planet A	Planet B	Planet C	You cannot tell

17. If all the planets orbit in the same amount of time which will be travelling the slowest?

1.	2.	3.	4.
Planet A	Planet B	Planet C	You cannot tell

18. Which planet is likely to have the hottest climate?

1.	2.	3.	4.
Planet A	Planet B	Planet C	You cannot tell

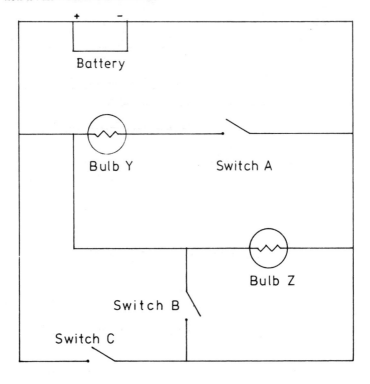

19. Which switch would you need to close in order to light bulb Y?

    1. Switch A
    2. Switch B
    3. Switch C

20. Which switch would you need to close to light both bulbs Y and Z?

    1. Switch A
    2. Switch B
    3. Switch C

21. Is it possible to light only bulb Z?

1.	2.	3.
Yes	No	Cannot tell

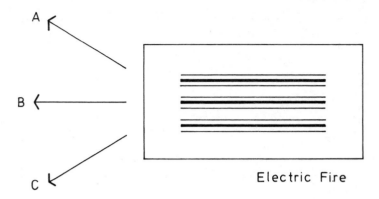

Electric Fire

22. In which direction would the convected heat travel?

1.	2.	3.	4.
A	B	C	All directions

23. In which direction would the radiated heat travel?

1.	2.	3.	4.
A	B	C	All directions

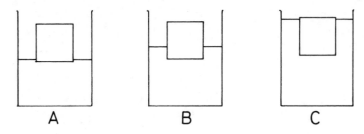

24. If in each instance the object consists of the same substance then which liquid has the greatest specific gravity?

1.	2.	3.	4.
A	B	C	They are all the same

25. If all three beakers contain identical liquids which object would be heaviest?

1.	2.	3.	4.
A	B	C	They are all the same

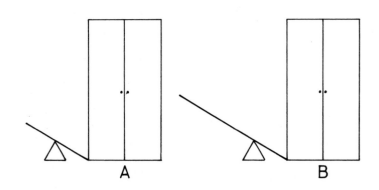

26. With which lever will it be easiest to lift the cupboard?

1.	2.	3.
A	B	Neither

A   B   C

27. If the fly wheels are rotated at the same speed which would be the hardest to stop?

1.   2.   3.
A   B   C

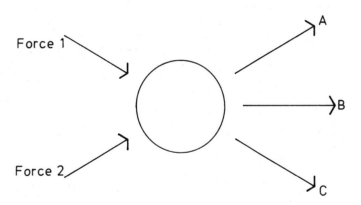

28. If force 1 and 2 are equal in which direction would the ball move?

1.   2.   3.
A   B   C

29. If force 1 is greater in which direction is the ball most likely to move?

1.   2.   3.
A   B   C

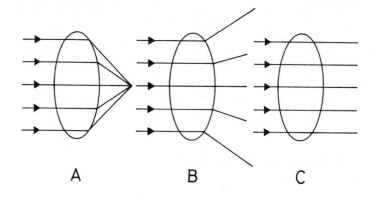

A   B   C

30. Which best illustrates the way in which light will be affected by the lens?

1.	2.	3.	4.
A	B	C	Neither

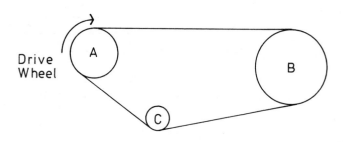

31. Which way will wheel B turn?

1.	2.
Anticlockwise	Clockwise

32. Which wheel will make the most revolutions in 60 seconds?

1.	2.	3.
A	B	C

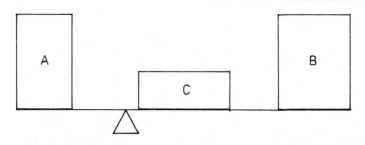

33. Which weight is the heaviest?

1.	2.	3.
A	B	C

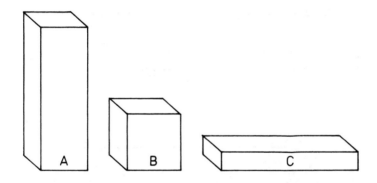

34. Which of these shapes is the hardest to turn over?

1.	2.	3.
A	B	C

Answers

Chapter 7: Technical verbal questions

1. C	2. C	3. A	4. D	5. B	6. A
7. C	8. B	9. B	10. C	11. D	12. A
13. E	14. E	15. C	16. D	17. A	18. C
19. B	20. C	21. D	22. C	23. A	24. C
25. B	26. A	27. E	28. C	29. A	30. E
31. C	32. C	33. E	34. A	35. A	36. C
37. D	38. E	39. C	40. A	41. C	42. B
43. E	44. D	45. C	46. C	47. A	48. D
49. B	50. D	51. A	52. B	53. B	54. D
55. B	56. A	57. A	58. E	59. B	60. C
61. B	62. E	63. A	64. C	65. A	66. B
67. A	68. A				

Chapter 8: Diagram reasoning questions

1. D	2. B	3. A	4. B	5. C
6. E	7. C	8. C	9. D	10. B
11. A	12. B	13. D	14. D	15. C
16. A	17. B	18. E	19. B	

Chapter 9: Mechanical questions

Section one (page 81)

1. (c)	2. (b)	3. (b)	4. (a)	5. (d)	6. (b)
7. (b)	8. (a)	9. (b)	10. (b)	11. (b)	12. (c)
13. (b)	14. (b)	15. (a)			

Section two (page 88)

16. 1	17. 3	18. 3	19. 1	20. 1	21. 1
22. 1	23. 4	24. 1	25. 3	26. 2	27. 3
28. 2	29. 3	30. 1	31. 2	32. 3	33. 1
34. 3					

Further Reading from Kogan Page

Great Answers to Tough Interview Questions, 3rd edition, Martin John Yate, 1992

How to Pass Computer Selection Tests, Sanjay Modhar, 1994

How to Pass Graduate Recruitment Tests, Mike Bryon, 1994

How to Pass Selection Tests, Mike Bryon and Sanjay Modha, 1991

How to Win as a Part-Time Student, Tom Bourner and Phil Race, 1990

How You Can Get That Job! Rebecca Corfield, 1992

Jobhunting Made Easy: A Step-by-Step Guide, 2nd edition, John Bramham and David Cox, 1992

Mind Mapping and Memory, Ingemar Svantesson, 1990

Preparing Your Own CV, Rebecca Corfield, 1990

Successful Interview Skills, Rebecca Corfield, 1992

Test Your Own Aptitude, 2nd edition, Jim Barrett and Geoff Williams, 1990